Also by David Lehman

POETRY

Valentine Place

Operation Memory

An Alternative to Speech


NONFICTION

The Last Avant-Garde
*The Making of the New York School of Poets*

The Big Question

The Line Forms Here

Signs of the Times
*Deconstruction and the Fall of Paul de Man*

The Perfect Murder
*A Study in Detection*


EDITED BY DAVID LEHMAN

The Best American Poetry (series editor)

Ecstatic Occasions, Expedient Forms
*85 Leading Contemporary Poets Select and Comment on Their Poems*

James Merrill
*Essays in Criticism (with Charles Berger)*

Beyond Amazement
*New Essays on John Ashbery*

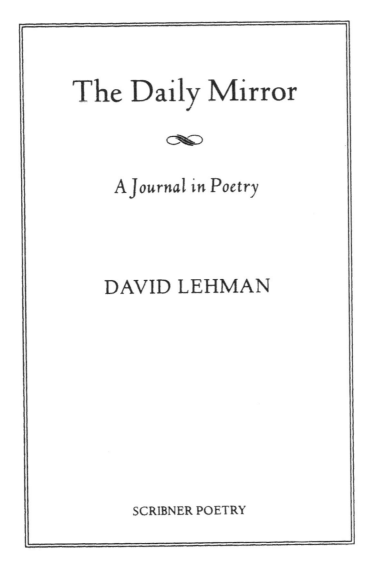

# The Daily Mirror

*A Journal in Poetry*

## DAVID LEHMAN

SCRIBNER POETRY

SCRIBNER POETRY
1230 Avenue of the Americas
New York, NY 10020

SCRIBNER POETRY and design are trademarks of Macmillan
Library Reference USA, Inc., used under license by
Simon & Schuster, the publisher of this work.

DESIGNED BY ERICH HOBBING

Manufactured in the United States of America

7   9   10   8   6

Library of Congress Cataloging-in-Publication Data

Lehman, David, 1948–
The daily mirror : a journal in poetry / David Lehman.
          p.     cm.
          I. Title.
    PS3562.E428D27     2000
    811'.54—dc21       99-37041
                CIP

ISBN 0-684-86493-2

# INTRODUCTION

In January 1996 I started writing a poem a day as an experiment. The initial results were hit-and-miss. Some poems didn't hit the spot, and I missed some days altogether. But I kept at it. Chronicling the progress of days seemed particularly worthwhile as I was then living in New York City, where every street corner seems to promise an adventure. I was also traveling a lot. I shuttled frequently to Ithaca, New York, where I own a house, and spent half of every January and June in Bennington, Vermont. Daily poems were written in these places and in San Diego, Cincinnati, Tampa, Boston, Miami, Albany, and Tulsa. I wanted to capture the excitement of travel and rapid change of scene in my poetry, and the daily poem offered a way to do that. It satisfied the wish to write about the particulars of experience and observation—to keep a sort of record of events, opinions, enthusiasms, dreams, fantasies, cravings, and thoughts, as they succeeded one another. At the same time the project provided a means to note the continuities in one's life. Many poems would be overtly about their specific occasions and implicitly about time and the calendar; the poem's title—in each case simply the month and day on which it was written—would see to that.

Toward the end of February inspiration hit big time. I began a consecutive day streak that reached 140. Writing a poem began to seem as natural as taking a walk. There were days when I wrote a sestina or a villanelle in addition to the official poem of the day. Waking up, I relished the thought that the day's poem waited to be written, as if it already existed in some ideal realm and needed only the tip of my wand to bring it to life. Poetry was, as one of the poems reported, a renewable energy source: the more you do it, the easier it gets, and the more enjoyable. Inspiration was not something you needed to sit and wait for. It was something that came when you invited it.

The practice of writing a daily poem has some of the advantages of keeping a journal but with a crucial difference: the desired end is an aesthetic product that asks to be read as a poem. The dailiness of the poems may act as a corrective to artificial poetic diction. It may keep the poem honest by rubbing its nose in the details of daily life. But however casual each poem may seem, however nonchalant, it has to work as verse—it must transcend the occasion of its making as only real poems do.

As to the specific occasion, the more diverse, the merrier. Some poems were written while I was talking on the phone, others while waiting for dessert at a restaurant. Several were composed in the form of E-mail messages, or on-line in "real time," like cybernetic epistles, a phrase that has the virtue of sounding like an oxymoron. I wrote a few while driving my car on the highway. All thirty poems written in April 1998 were posted one day at a time on the Web site of *Poetry Daily*, a venue as exemplary for my purposes as its name implies.

After two years I had the idea of making a book of these. Mindful of what Samuel Johnson said about *Paradise Lost* ("none ever wished it longer"), I decided against including one poem for each day of the year. My book would be selective but would nevertheless aspire to convey a sense of the calendar, the months, the seasons, the diurnal spin and the annual revolution: the Super Bowl gets played on the last Sunday in January, the vernal equinox occurs precisely on March 21, and the clocks spring forward on the first Saturday night in April. In culling the poems of several years and shaping them into a unity of one, I had the great example of Thoreau's *Walden* as my precedent.

The title of the book didn't occur to me until a few days after Frank Sinatra's last birthday was celebrated on December 12. Earlier titles had been proposed by Robert Polito ("The Best Days of the Year") and Archie Ammons ("Days of My Days"). On December 17, I told Donald Hall that I had finally settled on "Big City Daily," and then we both started refining that, and I can't remember which one of us said "The Daily Mirror" first. Bingo. *The Daily Mirror* was the name of a New York morning tabloid that went under as a result of the calamitous newspaper strike of 1962. (That strike ultimately also killed the *Herald Tribune*, the *World Telegram*

& Sun, and the *Journal-American*, though it did give birth to *The New York Review of Books*.) I liked the idea that a book of poems could call to mind not only an enchanted glass to be consulted daily, as by a princess in a fairy tale, but also a newspaper to be read by an impatient straphanger on the IRT.

From the start I valued speed of composition and was inspired by the idea that a theme or character introduced in one poem might pop up again. Some poems resemble monologues, employing personae. In others I am consciously thinking out loud, thinking on the run. We often take it for granted that reflection must precede poetry. Wordsworth said poetry was "emotion recollected in tranquillity," and the most important word in that formulation is *recollected*. Poetry is usually associated with memory, retrospect, an aftermath of contemplation succeeding the expiration of action. But the immediacy of American poetry, from Walt Whitman and Emily Dickinson onward, is one of its distinguishing characteristics. The daily poem, unpretentious as a diary entry, allows the poet to talk to the present. The practice also obliges him, inveterate daydreamer that he is, to be more attentive to his immediate surroundings—the music on the radio, the snow on the ground in the glitter of the sun—than he might otherwise be.

The discipline that the daily poem imposes speaks in its favor. It does wonders for your rate of productivity, and it promotes a willingness to take chances. Having accumulated so many poems, you are unlikely to prevent yourself from "wasting" one on a word game or a stunt that may, just may, turn into something worth perpetuating. You may as well try anything—a collage or cento, a "things to do" poem, a rhymed letter to a friend, a poem restricting itself to two words per line, an abecedarium. William Stafford, who wrote daily poems, was asked what he did when his poem of the day wasn't up to his usual standards. "Then I just lower my standards," he said.

There are other precedents besides Stafford. I think of Emily Dickinson (who wrote a poem every day in the years 1862 and 1863), of Frank O'Hara's "I do this I do that" poems, of James Schuyler's "June 30, 1974" and "Dec. 28, 1974," and of works by Ted Berrigan, Joe Brainard, A. R. Ammons, and most recently Robert Bly. The example of O'Hara meant the most to me, though it was Bly who pro-

7

vided the immediate impetus. Bly was a visiting lecturer at Bennington College, where I teach in the "low-residency" graduate writing program, during the frigid January session of 1996. He read us some of his daily poems, which he subsequently published under the title *Morning Poems* in 1997. Bly wrote his poems first thing in the morning, while still in bed, his dreams fresh in mind. I tried this method once or twice, with comical results; my own preferred time seems to be the late afternoon, though I've written some very late at night and others in the late morning.

One of the most compelling things about writing a daily poem is the feeling that a series of them will constitute a unified work composed of discrete parts that can stand on their own. Few ways of writing a long poem are as much fun. While there is some variation as to form, I experimented quite a lot with "skinny" poems, short lines, and in some cases little if any punctuation. In my previous book, *Valentine Place,* I used the past tense and the third-person point of view, so instinctively I favored the present tense and first-person here. It can't be a coincidence that as I was writing these poems, I was concurrently working on my book about the New York School of poets, *The Last Avant-Garde.* My recurrent themes seem to include love, sex, jazz, the twentieth century, poetry, movies, books, memory, friends and friendship, the weather, fathers and sons, and the city of New York.

# JANUARY 1

Some people confuse inspiration with lightning
not me I know it comes from the lungs and air
you breathe it in you breathe it out it circulates
it's the breath of my being the wind across the face
of the waters yes but it's also something that comes
at my command like a turkey club sandwich
with a cup of split pea soup or like tones
from Benny Goodman's clarinet my clarinet
the language that never fails to respond
some people think you need to be pure of heart
not true it comes to the pure and impure alike
the patient and impatient the lovers the onanists
and the virgins you just need to be able to listen
and talk at the same time and you'll hear it like
the long-delayed revelation at the end of the novel
which turns out to be something simple a traumatic
moment that fascinated us more when it was only
a fragment an old song a strange noise a mistake
of hearing a phone that wouldn't stop ringing

# JANUARY 2

∞

The old war is over the new one has begun
between drivers and pedestrians on a Friday
in New York light is the variable and structure
the content according to Rodrigo Moynihan's
self-portraits at the Robert Miller Gallery where
the painter is serially pictured holding a canvas,
painting his mirror image, shirtless in summer,
with a nude, etc., it's two o'clock and I'm walking
at top speed from the huddled tourists yearning to be
a mass to Les Halles on Park and 28th for a Salade
Niçoise I've just watched *The Singing Detective* all
six hours of it and can't get it out of my mind,
the scarecrow that turns into Hitler, the sad-eyed
father wearing a black arm-band, the yellow umbrellas
as Bing Crosby's voice comes out of Michael Gambon's
mouth, "you've got to ac-cent-tchu-ate the positive,
e-lim-inate the negative" advice as sound today
as in 1945 though it also remains true that
the only thing to do with good advice is pass it on

The shrink says, "Everything depends
on how many stuffed animals you had
as a boy," and my mother tells me my
father was left-handed and so is my son
and they're both named Joe whose favorite
stuffed animal was a bear called Sweetheart
while I, the sole constant in this dream,
am carrying a little girl who has a gun
in her hand as I climb a brick wall
on the other side is unknown territory
but it has to be better than this chase
down hilly streets where the angel disguised
as a man with red hair drives the wrong way
down a one-way street so he arrives late
at the library where his son is held hostage
he breaks in lifts the boy in his arms and tells
the one kind man he had met that he and
his brother would be saved but the others
who had mocked him would surely die

∞

Every time I hear
a new word I see
a new color, Joe
said in the cab. For
example, I said.
For example, he
said, the word
*example* is yellow,
brown, olive & a
little white mashed
together. And each
letter of the alphabet
has an age, a sex, &
a personality. H, for
example, is a lavender
girl, fourteen, a friend
of the number 4, who
is also a girl and also
lavender. And I? I
asked. I, he said,
is a genius, white.

# JANUARY 6

Lunch at Savoy (the
restaurant not the song,
"home of sweet romance,"
as done by Ella
and Louis) with Elliot
Figman who says they've got
a regular astrology column
in the redesigned *Poets*
*& Writers* I think they
should run a different writer's
horoscope each issue starting
with Richard Howard
a Libra and why
not have an evening with
James Merrill via the Ouija board
at the Algonquin we can ask
him whether he sees Elizabeth
and how Wystan is and did
he get the heavenly details
right in his book what do
you think Elliot

The day between
snow and sun like
the white and yolk
of a fried egg I wake
at three and shout
at my wife (who is
approximately 200 miles
and five years away)
because our son is
taking the new math
which in my dream means
living in a building without
walls or floors, hopping
from girder to girder,
and the sensation of falling
into a different century
all because someone
in December asked me
"how was your fall?"
and I said, "I'm still falling"
like the snow which stopped
when I woke up,
stretched, yawned,
read for three hours,
and took a walk in today's
blaze of white noon

Let's play Word Golf you go from
"love" to "hate" in fourteen lines
or from "kiss" to "fuck" one letter
at a time, like going from soft
to soot to loot to loft to lift
to life, that's my idea but Anne
Winters wants us to write a poem
ending with the line "and I die
of thirst at the fountain's rim"
so of course everyone does both
the snow like sea foam
surrounding a marooned sailor
stretches out before me, and how easy
it is for that mariner to swim
to shore a desert island where
he explores every inch on his belly
looking for water and dies
of thirst at the fountain's rim

∞

I have gone on an Arctic holiday
as a bit player in the pilot
of a new sitcom called *Blizzard*
on the Weather Channel I get
to recite an ode to the white wind
"O terrible white beauty," I say
"though seen by none save
the hooded figure in the landscape,
so absolute, point zero,
O dazzle of sunlight on snow!"
Those are my only lines.
They took days to learn.

# JANUARY 24

❧

I was about to be mugged by a man
with a chain so angry he growled
at the Lincoln Center subway station
when out of nowhere appeared a tall
chubby-faced Hasidic Jew with *payess*
and a black hat a black coat white shirt
with prayer-shawl fringes showing
we walked together out of the station
and when we got outside and shook hands
I noticed he was blind. Good-bye,
I said, as giddy as a man waking
from an anesthetic in the recovery room,
happy, with a hard-on. The cabs were
on strike on Broadway so beautiful
a necklace of yellow beads
I breathed in the fumes impossibly happy

# JANUARY 26

Freedom is wonderful
You can choose not to know
the names of actors and blues bands
or the teams playing in the Super Bowl
You can go to bed instead
of going to the movies
and if you're lucky the person
next to you will be you
of the curly locks what a coincidence
how sweet to think of all the routes
we have taken to arrive at this moment
and I wonder whether we were ever
in the same place at the same time
before we knew each other
and now good morrow to our waking souls
I am going to commit your scent to memory
and when you aren't here you'll still be here
and the person kissing you will be me

# JANUARY 31

The sky is crumbling into millions of paper dots
the wind blows in my face
so I duck into my favorite barbershop
and listen to Vivaldi and look in the mirror
reflecting the shopfront windows, Broadway
and 104th, and watch the dots blown by the wind
blow into the faces of the walkers outside
& here comes a thin old man swaddled in scarves,
he must be seventy-five, walking slowly,
and in his mind there is a young man dancing,
maybe seventeen years old, on a June evening—
he is that young man, I can tell, watching him walk

∽

Except for the food this is
a great restaurant, because
you're in it, my friend,
I'll have a double espresso
with a dollop of irony
and you'll have a Gershwin prelude
as we walk up Broadway
looking in vain for Edward Said
and ending up in Eden (Kathy's
office, that is) and if you pick up
the check I can promise you a top
job at my new magazine which I'm
thinking of calling *Peephole*
and we will print your limericks
about a certain great jazz bassist
who flew to Europe on Ireland's
national airline and knew what
his most valuable possession was

Intense, volatile, temperamental,
will not win amiability award or be
elected president of temple or club,
anxious to the point of taking action
in the form of needless phone calls
and letters to the editor, loses temper
on phone with staff underlings
and their bosses who call up
five minutes later to complain,
and thus is spent another glorious
morning on the job, stressed out,
pissed off, but still able to muster up
the old magic to explain why
one of the greatest sentences
of the twentieth century is,
"My mother was a saint"

∞

It used to be Garibaldi's, then it was Sardinia,
now it's Greek & it's still the worst restaurant
in the city, so naturally we go there instead of
*Suburbia* at the Angelika, & Robert orders
octopus, which is rank, while Lucie orders a
Greek salad. "Ugh," she says, because she
usually likes feta cheese but this stuff tastes like
goat cheese, which she hates. "But Lucie,"
I say, "feta cheese *is* goat cheese." She thinks
I'm joking. "Let's ask the waitress,"
Robert says. We bet the tab on it. And when
the waitress (name of Tricia) confers with her
colleagues, comes back with the hot chocolate,
and says, "The consensus is, we're not sure,"
I knew I had my poem of the day.

FEBRUARY 8

There are two kinds
of love songs:
"You're marvelous"
and "I'm heartbroken."
We live in the era
of the premature memoir
but I refuse to confess
or complain and when
you call I start singing
"Too Marvelous for Words"
instead of saying hello.
I'm not out of control.
I just flirt with everybody
because I love her.
The three of us
made a very disarming pair.

He was no altar boy
She was no chorus girl
He couldn't sit still
She couldn't drive
He couldn't sing
She couldn't stop
He wouldn't stop
She didn't say no
He hadn't planned to go
She wasn't born yesterday
He couldn't say
She wouldn't listen
He was no soldier
She was no nurse
It was no picnic

FEBRUARY 13

∾

It's Friday the 13th and I wonder
how the superstition got started.
I'd always thought it was because
there were thirteen diners at the
Last Supper but I recently saw a
documentary about the Knights
Templar according to which
King Philip of France mounted
a ruthlessly efficient surprise
attack on the Templars
and tortured them until they
confessed they were heretics,
gnostics. That happened on
a Friday the 13th in the 14th
century, and ever since it's been
an unlucky day to be caught
in a storm or shoplifting or in bed
with a person other than your mate
or just crossing the street before
looking both ways in New York
where, from one point of view,
it's always Friday the 13th

"Shocked," he agreed,
"but not surprised,"
and immediately I knew
I had to write a poem
ending with that phrase
pressure is what I need
I have twenty minutes to look
in the mirror and see the room
behind me, the bed, phone, lamps,
picture of an English foxhunt
on the wall, and now to ignore it
and focus on the face
in the mirror, the eyes the hair
the glasses that seem so much
a part of my face that when
I see a photo of myself without them
I'm shocked though not surprised

Light rain is falling in Central Park
but not on Upper Fifth Avenue or Central Park West
where sun and sky are yellow and blue
Winds are gusting on Washington Square
through the arches and on to La Guardia Place
but calm is the corner of 8th Street and Second Avenue
which reminds me of something John Ashbery said
about his poem "Crazy Weather" he said
he was in favor of all kinds of weather
just so long as it's genuine weather
which is always unusually bad, unusually
good, or unusually indifferent,
since there isn't really any norm for weather
When he was a boy his mother met a friend
who said, "Isn't this funny weather?"
It was one of his earliest memories

God is the cloud that
travels with my caravan,
Bessie Smith is in my living room
singing "Do Your Duty," and
I may look like a gas station attendant
but my name is Jackson Pollock
and I'm the Big Bang Professor
of theoretical physics
at Southern Comfort University,
and as a good citizen
of this fading century
whose rules of sexual engagement
were laid down by the Marquis de Sade
I know I am responsible for all I see
which I have organized
into cities and chambers
as one might organize the sea

# MARCH 2

When I think of her
Lynda Hull I hear Chet Baker's
boyish voice and see his face
like a crag funny each time
I fall in love it's always
you on the tape in the car
driving across the West Virginia
border that April morning
when Bill Wadsworth phoned me
to say she died in a car crash,
the violent death of choice
of the 1950s, and I hear "Cherokee"
with Bird on sax plus songs
he recorded when needing a fix
jazz is the music of the city but
you can take it with you
speeding across the border because
it's also the music of loneliness

# MARCH 4

∞

There's a potion I take
every day it contains echinacea,
osha, garlic, goldenseal,
ginger, chaparral, horse-
radish, usnea, cayenne,
and vodka I bought it in
Ithaca a place called Oasis
the bearded guy said his
wife made the stuff you
take it three weeks then
go off it and chew three
juniper berries every day
for a week I love Ithaca
when I'm not there in the
winter and my lilac bushes
are waiting for May
when I will come back
to admire them in full bloom

∞

The radio predicted snow,
wrong again, it's fifty degrees
but windy in the brisk sunlight
yesterday the owner of the Second
Avenue Deli was killed I had just
eaten there a pastrami and rye
sandwich with Dr. Brown's Cel-Ray
soda Abe (said to be "blustery"
in the *Times*) was taking the day's
till to the bank in his van
and was shot inside it or
outside and pushed back in
DiMaggio ate there as did Ali
I think of the Kosher delis
of my Yeshiva boyhood where
I went on days off for hot dogs
with mustard and sauerkraut
and then went home to watch
game two of the 1959 World Series
I hope they catch the son of a bitch
as another terrorist bomb goes off
in Israel I almost forgot
it's Purim

# MARCH 6

∞

I love sitting in bars in the Village
where the guy next to me says I love jazz
because Jews wrote the songs and blacks
sing them this time it's Ernie Andrews
and "Our Love Is Here to Stay" outside
it hasn't stopped raining, which makes
me want to dance like Gene Kelly (who
died last month) with Leslie Caron singing
the same song in *An American in Paris*
when I was an American in Paris
myself walking under the green lime trees
what a small city I could walk all the way
from Deux Magots to La Coupole and from
there to the Cité Universitaire at night
or in the morning with the workmen in blue
uniforms on the street the smell of
an omelette glass of red wine, and love
was easy an afternoon nap after the most
delicious charcuterie picnic the honking
horns orchestrated by Gershwin

# MARCH 9

Yesterday's version of today's flight
was cancelled but I'm going my life
couldn't be better the only problems
I have to solve are health
insurance, housing, and employment
other than that I haven't a care
the word *solve* has *love* in it,
I notice, and the aim of the day
is to end up in a poem like
this one in which four writers
a photographer an expert in Romanesque art
and a specialist in Chinese cinema
discuss the appeal of Tony Bennett
over sea bass (if that's what it was)
twelve flights above the Hudson River
you can sit by the window and paint it
or watch it dissolve into yesterday

MARCH 11

What common object
can be dialed on the phone
using only the numbers two and four?
hint: it is seven letters long
is it important like the night
I was asked my opinion of the painter
Jeff Koons and I pointed out
his name spelled backwards was Snook
and today with Nat Cole's silk voice
in my ear as I drive from Joe's school
where Andrea, the principal, tells me
she's taking a class in advanced astrology
she's a Libra but her moon in Scorpio
keeps her from being a wishy-washy type
I love Ithaca on mornings like this one
nothing like the sound of dripping water
that once was snow to cheer one up
and after watching *The Wild Bunch* last night
Joe said I'm going to write a sequel
to my philosophy of life and call it
*Brilliant Carnage*

∞

Every minute is vital
when day breaks in this bed
which contains the world
the lovers talk back to
the sun, "go wake up somebody
else," "I'm just doing my job"
some things don't shatter
when they break like the sleep
of refreshment it keeps on
breathing the cool air
with just enough moisture in it
eyes shut I know you are there
I like looking at my watch
in the dark when there are still
thirty minutes before the first
blast of espresso breaks my thirst
and the night sky breaks into
a clean flat slate of blue

Wisdom has the logic
of a haiku not a syllogism
the difference is spring
the light lasting longer
in March the month of mud
when hungry, eat
when angry, cool off
if a woman named Karen
comes to check your gas meter
do not jump her everyone's
in the mood I haven't seen a crocus
or a rosebud but "It Might As Well
Be Spring" on the radio
Archie phones and says
he's high on Coke which
in our private code means
he's bullish on Coca-Cola stock
which has already doubled and split
but just wait till they get to China

# MARCH 16

∞

The weather is on a lottery
system and I've lucked out two
Saturdays in a row it's warm
in Tampa where I want to eat
paella and smoke a cigar and
wonder if Tampax was invented
here I remember the year
my favorite song was "All of Me"
by Sinatra the phrase on everyone's
lips was "in your face" I wrote
odes to the nudes in Lee Friedlander's
photos the tropical tufts of pubic
hair and cheap alarm clocks
constantly going off as if time
were speeding up and the cabdriver
taking me to the airport said
I know you you're the guy who
played the doctor on *Love Boat*

# MARCH 17

Romance of palm trees
in the windy bay and you in
my bed that hurricane in the pillow
is your hair the color of Galliano
at the Valencia Bar the bottle was
so encrusted nothing would come out
"I keep telling him to get a new
bottle," says the bartender, and
"I didn't charge you for the club
soda and the coffee." Tip, tip,
and a five-spot for the Cuban
piano player playing "Perfidia"
her name is Margot as in Château
Margaux now it's one-twenty
in the afternoon Renee on the phone
says a winter storm is coming
midweek I'll worry about it later
for now the only storm I want
to think about is your golden hair

When spring comes I want to sit
on a bench in Washington
Square Park remembering when I
was a kid dreaming of being
a grown-up who gets to read
the paper on a park bench free
of anxiety, duty, responsibility
on a day when the temperature
is fifty-seven and "Blues for a
Dog" comes on WBGO and a friend
comes by in a white beard I
haven't seen since 1991 when
I was about to go to India he
had been there for a year he
said, would you like to go back
I said, he said he knew ex-cons
who'd like to go back to prison
for a weeklong visit if they could
that's how he felt about India

# MARCH 21

∞

The vernal equinox is to blame
for the celestial uproar, Anne
Carson said, and nothing surprises
me more than the streaks of white
sunlight this morning with Dexter
Gordon's version of "Tangerine"
in my mind the day is a rhyme
the pencil broke, no need to shout,
I want a girl to write sonnets about
in college & love is the food
that nourishes what it consumes
in springlike days in furnished rooms
I'm hungry, please come and touch me
and I'll whisper your name the only
thing missing in this picture is you

# MARCH 23

∾

Asparagus with prosciutto and
fettucine with salmon Arthur says
tragedy is the compulsion to repeat
as in *Oedipus Rex* and detective novels
and that's the key to an unhappy woman
we know but don't want to know
also Hitler as a repetition of Napoleon
I was in the tenth grade on the day
the Civil War began I mean November 22
1963 of course I love talking about
the century with Arthur and now it's time
to hop the #6 back to Astor Place
pick up a bottle of Fragonard and the mail
lie on the sofa reading Eric Ambler
and listening to Miles Davis, "Bags Groove,"
and then the sleep that surprises when you
turn off the lights to take a quick nap

MARCH 24

I remember England when sleep was
like a wrestling match with the sea
I dreamed my father had died and
when he did I dreamed he was alive
and woke up battered on the rocks
in any case twenty-five years ago
but today despite my nightmare of
an empty auditorium when I mount
the podium, I wake to let sleep
swallow me again, care-charmer sleep
with a comet glowing in the dark,
and a warm shower to wash the dust
out of my eyes, and the day begins
with "Do Nothing Till You Hear From Me"
jazz is the art of phrasing as
poetry is the art of timing what we
want from both is refreshment
we can never get enough of
let day be time enough to mourn
the shipwreck of my sea-tossed youth
I will listen to songs unlimited
in the deep dark chambers of sleep

I just heard a very fine
piano player described as
the General Motors of jazz
now why didn't I think of that
"but what does it mean?" you
ask who the hell knows the
sunlight's streaming through
the frayed yellowed curtains
in this flat that has grown
dear to me because I was sick
here and recovered as winter
is huffing and puffing its way
into spring the piano is playing
"Mona Lisa" in honor of the
Academy Awards last night I
stayed up for the whole dopey
thing and here's the light
of midday when the phone rings
I say "poetry headquarters"
making Hamilton laugh it's time

It's time for my hello
of the week: not a bellow
or a turgid novel by a Chicago-
based novelist (now in Boston), but a glow
in the dark of a firefly, a bee caught in the flow
of honey that sweetens the tea of my afternoon. O fellow
poet, spirit of the morning, with you I would dine on shad roe
and lie on a beach blanket and stare at your scarlet-painted toes
in the bright sunlight of July! To you I would present a rose
signifying beauty, and a pair of silk stockings (if hose
is called for, and it is), for I am in the throes
of contemplating you, my dear, and your charming nose,
ears, eyes, neck, eyelids, and hair. No more woes,
just the pleasure of a sentry saying "Who goes
there?" a question he likes to pose
of the universe, like the hellos
that link us in verse and prose

Nothing's greater than love unless
it's the primal urge to life
of the roaches in this apartment
but what do you mean by love
and how do you account for it
doesn't it come down to desire
yes the desire to fulfill
the desire of the beloved and
who is that voice singing "Time
After Time" did she say Annie
Ross the music by Jule Styne
never sounded so fine so lucky
to be loving you it exists in time
but not in space it charges
the morning even when the beloved
is absent or a variable or when
I first knew her when we drove
to a park and walked in the woods
beside a lake and came to a clearing
I couldn't believe my good fortune
sing it again time after time

∾

I had lunch with Robert Bly
the world's second best mumbler
after Marlon Brando it was
the exact day that spring succeeded
where winter had failed he told me
his doubts about Whitman and his
confidence in a kinesiologist in Florida
who can "read your body" over the phone
Ralph Waldo Emerson was on TV
when I got home he was urging
viewers to invest in God by calling
1-800-Judaism and suddenly I knew what
was American about American poetry
as opposed to the Europeans, who were
too busy writing love letters to God
to notice whether Death was a man or woman

∞

In *The Best Years of Our Lives*
the frank and friendly smile
of Dana Andrews who couldn't get
a job despite his Distinguished
Flying Cross he was my idea
of what a grown-up man should
look like wearing a tie with
his bomber jacket, a soda jerk
in a drugstore, and a double-
breasted suit to his pal's wedding
one of the fallen angels
of the air force why is it when
I go to the movies today I
rarely believe the male lead
is a grown-up in the old-fashioned
sense of fathers who went to work
downtown every morning is it
because I'm one of them now
when I wanted to be Dana Andrews
in *Zero Hour* or William Holden
in *Executive Suite* those were the days

Every errand's a fool's errand
if we run it because
I'm a fool to want you
and you're a fool to agree
that's an example of a sonnet
in four lines
on a day when human folly
is celebrated with pranks when
what's needed is a grin
such as the angels sport when
regarding us from the clouds
what they see are donkeys
with big ears, horses whinnying,
frog leapfrogging on frog
that's us in their eyes
at the moment we think
we resemble angels on levitating beds

What I like about reading in the dark is
you can't see what you're reading
and must imagine verses equal to your longing
and then Keats shows up with "La Belle Dame
Sans Merci" and Yeats wonders whether
"you" will ever be loved for yourself alone
and not your yellow hair
when I was a Columbia freshman
we had to compare those two poems
I wish I were asked to do that today
for I have finally figured it out
but at the time all I could think to say
was that both women, the one whose eyes
were shut with kisses four
and the one with the yellow hair,
were the same woman, and I knew her

∞

I like movies like dreams that
jumble the order of events
there is no past in a dream
everything is happening now
so you can be married and
divorced and still be the boy
whose father took him to see
*How to Succeed in Business*
*Without Really Trying* with
Michele Lee as Rosemary in 1965
two years later I was reviewing
plays for the Columbia *Spectator*
it's fun to write about something
you know nothing about like
*Rosencrantz and Guildenstern*
*Are Dead* I forget what was wrong
with it but something was that's
what criticism is "all about"
plus a few remarks about parody,
chance, and the absurd, just as
poetry is "all about" time which
equals love times death squared

# APRIL 4

∞

Fire engines in St. Mark's Place
Larry Rivers on saxophone
painting a man in formal evening clothes
spanking a beautiful Boucher bottom
with nylons and heels while I
photocopy the 1950s on your machine
the women eating soup at the counter
of B & H Dairy look even better
now that I've seen them nude on your walls,
dear Larry, who taught me how to see
French money and the Cedar Tavern menu
I must leave you now, yon water tower beckons
me to the roof where the sky retains its blue
as darkness descends in the empire of light
on Thirteenth Street and First Avenue

APRIL 5

Bill and Jaye are on their way
to San Francisco, birthplace
of Robert Frost, author
of "Birches," well, one could do
worse, I too have been
halfway to heaven and back
on the swing of a birch tree
though there aren't any birches
in San Francisco, I don't think,
which is where they're going,
Bill and Jaye, to kick off
National Poetry Month with
Thom Gunn, Adrienne Rich (we hope;
she had a fall last month and is
on the mend), poet laureate Bob
Hass and others do I wish I
could be there no I like it here
in New York where Sarah wants
to go see the abstract show
at the Guggenheim and Amy Hempel
is reading on Easter Sunday there'll
be a party afterwards Robert will be there
as will I with a poem in my pocket

## APRIL 6

She's a high-maintenance doll
at two in the morning she starts
talking the pauses between your
answers grow longer she says
"you're not listening" you repeat
what she said she says "that's
just a trick you weren't really
listening" and before you know it
you're snoring in her ear a version
of "I Wished on the Moon" by Billie
Holiday and the moon slips under
the sea chased by a whippet
who is licking your neck ah fidelity
to wake up and she's still there
there is something to be said
in favor of five hours of sleep
on this Saturday when the clocks
spring forward and you spring into
action because she wants her coffee
and no one else is in on the secret

APRIL 8

∞

Maybe Jim Cummins and I
will write *John Ashbery
for Dummies*. Maybe I'll
move to Paris for ten years
and still speak with a New
York accent. Maybe I'll
make a movie about three
feckless French women in
their late twenties, each
of whom quits her job in
a provincial city to come
to Paris. Maybe I'll learn
whether French women
in bras and panties look
different from their U.S.
counterparts and, if so,
is it because of their
garments or their diet?
Maybe I'll while away
the afternoon walking
until evening in a café
where I'll take out my
notebook to write,
"I haven't written
a poem in months."

# APRIL 9

I woke up not in Paris
that's the first thing that went wrong
after the pleasure of a week
of speaking French badly
also the smoke detector went off
when I made coffee,
and my telephone lacks a dial tone
so I know I'm back in the greatest city
with my incomparable view of garbage
in the alley out the window with sun
a bright white on red brick turning yellow
and just enough blue to imply a sky
high enough and far enough away
to stand for all that's mind (mine)

∞

My name, if I were French,
would be Jean-Louis
and if I were Frank and you
were Grace Kelly I'd sing
"You're Sensational" before
my big duet with Bing
I think I'll go get a haircut
and celebrate by dozing
off in the barber's chair
but what are you celebrating
well let's see there's that
amazing bottle of red wine
(Château Calon-Ségur
St.-Estèphe Médoc, 1988)
Bill and I quaffed at Sarah's
there's the expression on your
face when I photographed you
in the bathtub there's spring
which came a month early
this year but is sticking around
for the celebration

# APRIL 13

I threw away the script
(Greater than poetry is the rain)
Then let you take my arm who were
the calm before the cigarette
and I was its eye and you
had to leave but I had to stay
and then she asks "poetry"
and he answers yes but
he loves "the liquefaction of her
clothes" more than the words
which acquire their value only
after she leaves and takes
her beautiful zaftig body which has
gone from Brooklyn to Barnard
with her and he is alone
with Graham Greene who proves
that Catholicism exceeds all other
religions in the erotic delight
the sin of adultery delivers
well goodnight thanks for coming
no thanks for having me

The summer I worked
in the post office
all the carriers were
nervous wrecks who
had gone to Vietnam
and fathered children with
Vietnamese prostitutes
I saw their hands shake
there must be a reasonable
explanation there must
and made up my mind right
there I wouldn't go no
matter what it was 1967
and the Spanish girl who
opened the door when I
delivered the parcel had
black hair brown eyes and
nothing on beneath her slip

What a sweet guy I am
when one of my enemies dies
I don't Xerox the obit and mail it
to the others saying "Let
this be a lesson to you," no
I'm more likely to recall
the person's virtues to which I
was blind until the news of mortality
opened my mind as you would
open a vial of Tylenol noticing
it spells lonely backwards with
only the initial T added, signifying
taxes no doubt, and now my headache
has gone the way of leaves in fall
am I happy I certainly am
as you would be, my friend, if
the Queen of Sheba returned your calls
as she does mine

∞

Do I think you should wear
your hair up or down? I think
up would be nice it would show
your face but down is how you
have it now curling wildly
around you I like it like that
and the way you start singing
as we walk up MacDougal Street
and stop at the corner of West
Third to hear whose sax is
sending notes up in the air
where they linger before the wind
wafts them with us to Sixth Avenue
where you resume your song
in a cab while I walk solo
to the Larchmont Hotel no heat
in this cold April night and
the shower is a skinny trickle
of warm water but I'm as happy
as Susannah McCorkle singing
"Who Wants to Be a Millionaire?"

Jorie Graham is waiting
at the Knickerbocker just in
from West Point where she
reviewed the troops and
the concept of just and unjust
wars she'll have a gin and tonic
I'll go for a Tanqueray martini
the question is whether *The
Iliad* is for or against war
Jorie puts on a black
spangled scarf and the van
takes us to Seton Hall where
she reads her poem "Concerning
the Right to Life" afterwards
she's still talking about the cadets
the discipline in the first year
when their names are taken from them
and how serious they are when they
read Hemingway it's because they may
need that information they have
agreed to take a life
or give one up in exchange
for this marvelous free education

I'm a very average person,
and I think most people are.
I vote with the common man.
I have two kids, a boy and a girl.
Last Sunday I played golf with the boss.
Hey, it beats working.
I'm his wife. I may be brainless but
I'm her husband. I played golf with her
Last Sunday I played golf with the boss
and it was the first warm morning in May
and like every other moron driving a lawn mower
I'm their husband. I may be brainless but
I'm their wife. I'm their mother.
I have two kids, a boy and a girl,
and it was the first warm morning in May
and I think most people are
like every other moron driving a lawn mower.
I'm a very average person.
I vote with the common man.
Hey, it beats working.

# APRIL 23

The birthday of Vladimir
(rhymes with redeemer)
Nabokov coincides with
Shakespeare's and yours,
old pal, so I spend
this gray morning with
the skyline as lovely in
the rain and fog as Chartres
when you first espy it
from the passenger seat of
a yellow rented Renault,
"you" in this case being
someone else again from
the first "you" in this poem,
though I remain the same
guy who winked at you
in the street this morning.
Once again I have
willed us to France for
the length of a cab
ride to La Guardia. No
breakfast but the strongest
espresso, and instead of an
alarm clock, your pretty voice.

America you are not getting any younger
looking less like T. S. Eliot each day
you would rather play volleyball
on the beach than listen to mermaids
the average age of the citizenry remains 18
and we would burn our draft cards
at the campfire singing "If I Had a Hammer"
in Spanish except that there are no draft cards
left they're like the baseball cards
the mothers of America threw out when
their sons went to college and took the pills
that would keep them young forever
in New York, where everyone's in a hurry,
and I walk fast to keep inconspicuous
and look like I know where I'm going
to find you the way a sailor on his one-day leave
finds a woman to marry and never see again

When my father
said *mein Fehler*
I thought it meant
"I'm a failure"
which was my error
which is what
*mein Fehler* means
in German which
is what my parents
spoke at home

As Hamlet would have said
if he had lived through
the Russian Revolution and
his author had written in Russian,
"To live a life is not to cross
a field." I think I see what he
means, or would have meant,
by that line so hard to translate,
yet I wouldn't underestimate
the difficulty of crossing a field,
a snow-covered expanse, say,
wide as the Steppes, that no
footprints have defaced, so that,
staring at it, you feel like
a writer facing a blank page,
and the trees may be full of rifles,
and the whole reason for crossing
the field escapes you now that
you have reached its edge,
and the rumor of a castle
on a high hill in the distance
is almost certain to turn out false.

# APRIL 29

God bless Wellbutrin
I see the market's down
a hundred and forty points
but I don't care I know
it will go up again tomorrow
thanks to the Dead Cat Bounce
as "the Street" terms it
still I refuse to invest in El Niño
by buying soybean futures
on the Chicago Options Exchange
I'd rather phone Joe who answers,
"You have reached WJOE,
all Joe Lehman, all the time,"
as for the guy who reviewed Jim
Tate's book and called it "almost
Victorian in its piety," I got news
for you, buddy, not even the Victorians
were Victorian in their piety have you
ever read "In Memoriam" or "Dover Beach"
well, have you, punk?

To speak no more to be able,
To die might better it be, and I
To the opera on Sunday may
(If opera for funeral you say) fly,
So sorry for every evil person
In history feel I. With them
What wrong went when I think
That they to kill everybody wanted.
Pain what. Mind my lost I.
Hammer in the night, so hungry, why
I have, without it your knowing,
Babbling started, part the worst is, and,
When on you work they. What
Could have they been, that is.

## MAY 2

∞

Someday I'd like to go
to Atlantic City with you
not to gamble (just being
there with you is enough
of a gamble) but to ride
the high white breakers
have a Manhattan and listen
to a baritone saxophone
play a tune called "Salsa
Eyes" with you beside me
on a banquette but why
stop there let's go to
Paris in November when
it's raining and we read
the *Tribune* at La Rotonde
our hotel room has a big
bathtub I knew you'd like
that and we can be a couple
of unknown Americans what
are we waiting for let's go

# MAY 3

∞

Let's say we go to Amsterdam,
the Venice of the North,
or Venice, the Amsterdam
of the South, and Florence,
the Paris of the Italian Renaissance,
with a stop at Padua as Giotto
imagined it, a totality of blue, or Paris
on a windy day in March,
kind of blue in the Miles Davis manner
with streaks of white and just a little bronze
and just about now Peggy Lee
starts to sing "He's a Tramp,"
I like the way she breathes,
the way you look, as we swim
in Menton (the Newport of the French Riviera,
or has it moved back to Nice?), and it's time
to decide to drive to Italy for lunch
with good wine I prefer Delacroix
on the hundred franc note while you hold out
for Cézanne and his apples, blue and green,
as if we were young and rich
before we were born

## MAY 6

The brain has chambers
on different floors
a warren of offices
upstairs a library
a wine cellar below
but the soul is simple
like a mother who
packs your lunchbox
and you walk home
wearing the raincoat
she made you take
though it is sunny
and mild my mother
when I was four was
talking to another
mother and I strayed off
and went to the park
and found someone to
walk me home where I sat
on a car waiting for
her to come back she was
frantic but when she saw
me she laughed the soul
is a hungry boy eating
her soup in the kitchen

∞

700 francs will get you $109.91
on this muggy May afternoon
which is good to know since
I just found 700 francs in my wallet
while Dinah Washington was singing
"My Old Flame" I was thinking of where
I was with Glen when Allen Ginsberg died
and if I could relax for one hour
if I knew what that felt like
it would seem like a very long time to me
so I'll have to settle for the next best thing
warm rain on a cool May evening
on Charles Street, turn left on West 4th,
cross Sixth and turn right on MacDougal
quick: make a sentence that has Spike Lee
Son of Sam and Leonardo DiCaprio in it
Bob Dole says Viagra is a great drug
that's the news, the weather I've already
given you, and then I want to go
into the bedroom and find your naked body
in my bed you've stayed up waiting for me
and I'm going to make it worth your while

Joe finished his paper
on ethics he liked Socrates
("all I know is I don't
know anything") and Plato
("the ideal dog is Lassie")
but aren't you still in the
cave, Joe, yes, watching
shadows on a screen thinking
they're the real thing when
I was twelve I knew nothing
about Socrates except that
he died drinking hemlock
but I liked the idea of
philosophy for example what
to do if you see someone cheat
and it's your best friend
I know what E. M. Forster says
but I still haven't solved it

# MAY 10

∞

The best way to learn a foreign language
is to go to the place and rent a car
with a little Berlitz phrase book
In every language there's one sentence
the tourist must learn
In Italian it's Excuse me where's the church
of Santa Maria della Vittoria
In French it's Do you have any brake fluid?
In German it's What did I do wrong?
In English it's I'm sorry to have to tell you
that Gerry Freund died
and there's nothing you can do about it
you can't phone him up to say
you'll miss him

I spend a half hour comparing
Cliff Robertson of the pained face
in *Obsession* with James Stewart
in *Vertigo* one difference is
the former gets her (Genevieve
Bujold) back only now she's his
daughter both movies are mind-
fucks in the positive sense (is
there any other?) Larry Joseph
phones and says he hears I'm
going to be the guest host
of "What's That Line" at
the poetry game show next week
in New York I can't deny it I'm
going to lie on my couch in vacant
or in pensive mood and summon up
some lines I love for the joy
of saying them out loud my heart
aches my genial spirits fail the lone
and level sands stretch far away
and after many a summer dies the swan

∞

A book could be written
on the moment swing turned
into bop the moment Lester
Young, Roy Eldridge, and
Teddy Wilson gave way to
Bird, Dizzy, Miles, Bud,
and Monk in fact it would
be a great movie at least
the sound track would be
"beyond category" as Duke
Ellington would have put it
the life of a jazz musician
(about which I know so little)
is the life for me I felt
on the afternoon Jamie and I
visited his father who sat
at the piano and talked and
played I was tongue-tied and
wanted him to play a song
as if Helen Merrill were there
and her voice and his fingers were
about to have an intimate talk

## MAY 14

On street corners in Hiroshima
a machine plays a tune to let
blind people know the light
is green and here I am with
a pad in my hand listening to
the presidents of Harvard,
Brown, and Duke deplore recruitment
practices on their campuses
would you say these men are sincere
I would unhesitatingly do so
each is married to the mother
of the girl I was in love with
when this day began four years
ago and then my father turned up
and said Hitler would soon come back
and when he does what will you be
doing, writing poetry? This went on
for an hour then he said enough
about the world tell me about Mama
while I tried to figure out who
this imposter was who claimed to be
my father, dead since 1971

Sinatra, snapping out of a haze,
noticed me sitting across from him
"Who the fuck are you?"
Just another fan, I said, on the day he died
I made anagrams out of his name
satin, sin, stain, stair, train, rain, star
and figured out my last message
I mean what I would say to him now
your good-bye left me with eyes that cry
on the other hand you left me the history
of your voice the record of the American century
from Roosevelt to Reagan you will live on
whenever I need to hear you (it has to be you)
sing "I Get Along Without You Very Well"
(Strand's favorite) or "I'm a Fool to Want You"
(my choice) when your lover has gone

Fifty-two degrees light rain
and a thirty-minute delay at
the Midtown Tunnel I'm back
giving thanks I'm not in
publishing and don't have
to read another memoir
of a dysfunctional family
the difference between me
and that homeless guy
talking to himself on
thirty-sixth street is
I'm going to the Poetry
Game Show tonight and if
somebody heckles me
I'm going to tell
the guy his works
will be read long after
Shakespeare's have been
forgotten
but not until then

I read Byron's recipe for a hangover
and Jennifer Cahill guessed it was
by Charles Bukowski and I said Byron
would turn over in his grave and
somebody else guessed Dylan Thomas
and I said Lord Byron isn't read much
I see and somebody finally said
Byron right for five points at
the Poetry Game Show where Siobhan
of the Academy of American Poets
dons a bikini and a hat the shape
of a slab of Swiss cheese to read
a Stevie Smith poem about wearing
a weird hat on a desert island
we go to the Knickerbocker you stand
I sit at the glass bar there's
Dick Katz whose new CD is called
"The Line Forms Here" a title I
love so much I used it for a book
in 1992 and as for the future
I say the future is a serious matter
and so for God's sake hock and soda water

We want change
but we don't want to change
sometimes you don't want to hear a voice
a trumpet is enough with bass and drums
motors and horns bass and drums
motors and horns the repetition
makes it a song though the melody
may be hard to pick up the day is like that
the war is over the soldier returns home
in no mood to argue with well-meaning journalists
swilling the scotch in raucous bars or was that
the last war yes the generals are always one
war behind but that needn't detain us
we don't need someone to explain us
this is our music, it's not supposed to entertain us
or train us for a constructive cultural role
it's just ours to keep to ourselves if we like
in public places looking inconspicuous

Movies are meant to be seen
when you're alone especially
when you're living in England
and wishing you were in France
so you go to *Le Bonheur* and
memorize the dialogue then you go
to France and see American films
and study the French subtitles
which teach you how to behave
it's enjoyable to make
global generalizations on
the basis of haphazard observations
the English value gardening over cooking
ergo their idea of wickedness is
bad manners while the French
idea of wickedness is bad taste
and in the movie the man kissing the woman
says "don't believe me though
I never lie" I've always wanted to say
that to a girl if I tell you
I love you don't believe me

# JUNE 1

The new day (a gray streak
of light) begins with
the bubbles still in
last night's soda water
in my glass by the bed
I've got to pack pick up
a rental car load it and
drive up to Ithaca it'll be
good to be in the big house
but I don't want to leave
hard as it is to live in
this city I'm still a sucker
for the lights of Amsterdam
Avenue the bright yellow of
taxis in snow I feel like
a runner with a big lead off
first base who slides into second
and when the catcher's throw
skips into center field he hustles
to third his uniform streaked
with dirt he's safe

# JUNE 5

If I write another
poem about Ithaca
let it be called
"Chance of a Shower"
no Korean restaurant
dispenses cherry
lime rickeys here
but if you bring
the white crème de
menthe I'll meet you
halfway with brandy
and make us stingers
you saw an osprey
a kingfisher two
red-tailed hawks
and four blue herons
in the Dryden wetlands
Renee you've become
quite a birdwatcher
and if a friend calls
and says "we've got
to talk" it can mean
one thing only you
haven't won the lottery

∞

No two are identical though
they begin from the same
point in time the same point in
the dream when the radio shuts
itself off in the middle of
"Just in Time" (Sinatra version)
the curtains are blowing in
and the driver of the hearse
outside looks up and says "Room
for one more" and now you
know what kind of hospital you're in
and you must escape from it
by acting "normal" pretending there isn't
a conspiracy against you as *Dead of Night*
shifts into *Shock Corridor*
there are a dozen versions of this dream
I keep thinking of what Ashbery said
about escapism he said we need
all the escapism we can get
and even that isn't going to be enough

# JUNE 8

It's three days before my birthday
I think I'll rent *Doctor Zhivago*
tonight (Hilton Obenzinger said
he liked the music) and read the novel
today and write a poem tomorrow about
the Russian Revolution as performed
by the students of Columbia College
in 1967 Michael Steinlauf had a beard
David Shapiro a mustache Les Gottesman
went to Poland for the summer
and Hilton Obenzinger bought a pound
of ground chuck and walked to Hamilton Hall
where a class on Plato was in progress
he threw the meat into the room
yelled "Meat!" and ran away

∞

Nothing like a little English rain
on a humid American afternoon
I think I will write a one-line
"Language" poem here it is
it's called "Syntax" and the line
is "Sin tax" and now you may
ponder the example (formerly ample)
of a dime on every cigarette
a dollar for each tilting highball
enforcing the smug puritanism
that succeeded the desperate hedonism
that followed the guarded optimism
of grammar school enough of that
I'm in adjectival bliss & it's
time for recess & how I studied
the unreflecting windows in
that high classroom

# JUNE 10

∞

The sun like whiskey and caffeine
goes right to your head
slowing you down then speeding you up
you spend one hour looking at three
hanging plants and ten minutes
reading the obits lamenting the man
(I knew him, we had Irish Coffee
one cold December night)
who had the ill fortune to die
on a day when somebody really famous
like the leader of a rock band
died and so his obituary was overlooked
and I am thinking of him today
I'd tip my cap to him if I were wearing one
but I'm not I'm standing here
unprotected in the sun
that has gone to my head like a song

It's my birthday I've got an empty
stomach and the desire to be
lazy in the hammock and maybe
go for a cool swim on a hot day
with the trombone in Sinatra's
"I've Got You Under My Skin"
in my head and then to break for
lunch a corned-beef sandwich and Pepsi
with plenty of ice cubes unlike France
where they put one measly ice cube
in your expensive Coke and when
you ask for more they argue with
you they say this way you get more
Coke for the money showing they
completely misunderstand the nature of
American soft drinks which are an
excuse for ice cubes still I wouldn't
mind being there for a couple of
days Philip Larkin's attitude
toward China comes to mind when
asked if he'd like to go there he said
yes if he could return the same day

JUNE 14

∾

This is the saddest story I ever
heard about the oncologist who has
good news and bad news the bad news
is he's going to die the good news
is he's fucking his nurse Liam
reads the first sentence of *The Good Soldier*
out loud and Jason guesses it's from
*The Day of the Locust* by F. Scott Fitzgerald
a brilliant idea Jason I think you
should write it and also *Gatsby* as
Nathanael West would have done it
a tale of passion in the still of the night
where Sven, Doug, Askold and I drink wine
and argue about Kissinger, McNamara,
long-range killing and the need to make
distinctions between MacArthur and Ike
may I have a cigarette sure I didn't
know you smoke well I just started
but I won't deny it it's been wonderful

# JUNE 16

∽

It's Bloomsday in Dublin
and wherever Ulysses works
as an advertising man
with an unfaithful wife
as I sit here listening
to a lecture on Flannery
O'Connor, Frank O'Connor,
and the O'Hara boys, John
and Frank, I think of going
to Dublin with you buying
a toy wedding ring at
Woolworth's and the phrase
"mock funeral" comes
to me I don't know what it
means though I remember being
the groom at a mock wedding
with a girl named Ann in 1956
I was eight and so was she
and all the other children
were in the procession it was
the first hot night in June and
yes she said yes I will Yes

# JUNE 19

∞

Ella Fitzgerald died
and I haven't had a minute to cry
about it but I listened to her
driving here and I'll be listening to her
driving back home I'll play
the Irving Berlin Songbook and then
Rodgers and Hart, "The Lady Is a Tramp,"
but not this lady Ira Gershwin said
"I never knew how good our songs were
until I heard Ella Fitzgerald sing them"
the queen of scat oh Ella I hope
you and Billie Holiday are comparing
notes in heaven right now
while I am back on earth hearing you sing
"It Was Just One of Those Things"

## JUNE 27

On the slope a white man said
he could cure cancer and a big
black man in manacles was led
to a pool of water and placed in it
I had two apartments and in both
I had an extra room I offered one
to Glen he accepted I looked in
a drawer, deciding what to pack,
and found brand-new shirts imported
from Italy never removed from their
wrappers one was a green plaid
sportshirt though the illustration
on the label showed a man wearing
the shirt with a solid green tie
I was back in summer camp only now
I was bringing my own son
and the camp was a hospital
and the kids were playing ball games
as if nothing out of the ordinary
had happened I went back inside
and packed, thinking you haven't
left until you pack and I was leaving

∞

This one's for you, Nin,
on whom I shall confer
a doctorate of love now
that you've won your master's
in Eros and your bachelor's
in Aphrodite what's left is
the banquet at which Diotima
teaches the old men to see
though drunk the daughters
of memory and Socrates who can
drink everyone under the table
gets to walk her to her doorstep
and kiss her lightly on the lips
showing he has failed to learn
her latest lesson but who cares

# JUNE 30

Don't walk away, Renee,
I'm just getting warmed up
your body is like a river
and I'm going to swim across
I want to explore the left
bank of you then the right
you're the only woman in
this room with a sunflower
in her hair and you take
forever in the bathroom
making me wait finally you
emerge with a bottle of beer
in one hand an ashtray in
the other and say, "OK, when
do we start?" you're looking
good tonight Renee with about
twenty-five bracelets on your
left wrist bandages on both legs
an ankle bracelet how I long
to see you wearing nothing but
that ankle bracelet all my poems
are about you tonight Renee

## JULY 6

∽

Your Honor I object
objection overruled counselor you may
proceed to unmask the witness
the witness will please answer the question
where were we at nine o'clock on the sixth
we were in a sleeping bag on a field
under the big dipper the little dipper
the planets and the moon
and I'm still trying to make sense of what happened
to us that night
the thoughts that go through a man's mind
when he lies in bed sleepy while the woman
in the shower is singing and he knows
she's happy with her hair wet and full of suds
he will sneak in with a grin and cop a peek
that's not a federal offense, is it?
but how do you explain her disappearance
I wish I could answer that question
I honestly can't remember how I got here
or where that star-filled field went
thank you your witness

∞

The phone. "Dodgers' locker room,"
I answered. It was the late Oscar
Hammerstein inviting me to enter
his AOL chat room devoted to the lyrics
of Lorenz Hart. What a great day
this is, I thought. Then I drank
the juice of three oranges and ate
the greatest-tasting yogurt of all time,
Meadowsweet brand, Sun Nut flavor.
Then Thelonious Monk played for me
and I thought of Claudia who heard
wrong and thought it was The
Loneliest Monk at the piano:
"Well, You Needn't," "Bemsha Swing."
Nobody wants to be existential anymore,
though it isn't a bad life, I thought as I
drove to Wegman's, parked my red Corolla
(she'll be nine in October) and walked into
the supermarket that won the Cold War

The sky was a midnight blue
velvet cloth draping
a birdcage and no moon
but the breeze was whistling
and the sound of a car
on Valentine Place was
the rush of a waterfall
on the phone in New York City
and that's when the muse
turned up with curly brown locks
she was a poet, too, and wanted
me to give her an assignment
she was willing to trade
fifteen minutes of inspiration
in return for a phone call
from Frank O'Hara in heaven
sipping espresso and Irish whiskey
and then a morning swim
we had so much energy those days
we needed to burn some up
before we could paint

# JULY 11

You propose a picnic
I will choose the wine
you will pick the place
he and she will not replace
us no for the sake of our love
I will rent a car in Paris
and meet you in Cerbères
and you will pack a basket
with simple things like
bread and cheese and jam
they will be watching
and you will wonder who "they"
are and I won't be able to
tell you it will be a kind of
test but we're too busy
kissing to notice or care
failure is not a possibility
I like what's in your basket

Wisteria, hysteria is as obvious a rhyme
as Viagra and Niagara there must be a reason
honeymooners traditionally went to the Falls
which were, said the divine Oscar,
an American bride's second biggest disappointment
tell me which do you like better,
the American Falls or the Horseshoe Falls,
I say the Horseshoe Falls, Joe says,
because its magnificence surpasses the American Falls
thank you, Joe, and did you know
when Casey Stengel managed the Yankees
he sat next to Bob Cerv on the bench one day,
put his arm around the big outfielder, and said,
"One of us has just been traded to Kansas City"
I don't know what put that in my mind
except that it backs up Michael Malinowitz's line
about John Ashbery being the Casey Stengel of poetry
meanwhile the Yankees are playing like the Bronx Bombers of old
and though I used to hate the Yankees I'm just enough
of a New York chauvinist to feel gleeful about it
wait a minute I'll be right back I am back that's
another line I've always wanted to put in a poem
what it will say on Johnny Carson's gravestone
"I'll be right back"

I'm going to miss you, Robert Mitchum,
as I make my rounds in lower Manhattan
checking the progress of Joe DiMaggio's
56-game hitting streak the way you did
in *Farewell, My Lovely.* Next to Bogart
you were the best Philip Marlowe. Smart,
too. Getting arrested for marijuana use the
year I was born was a shrewd career move.
Sleepless by instinct, you looked like
a car mechanic and were a fighter whose best
moment came when he got off the canvas
and took another punch. You lost every fight
with the woman in the houseboat who sang
"There's a fire down below in my heart."
She came out of the past and now at last
you've joined her in some South American
beach where escaped convicts dream
of going, and I'm walking on Sixth Avenue
with your groggy voice in my mind
daring the world to surprise you.

Just as a company's closing stock price today
reflects expert estimates of its future earnings,
so, in the economy of the psyche,
anxiety is the fear of future unhappiness,
and as desire always exceeds its fulfillment
disappointment is inevitable that's my theory
of surplus desire as for insomnia
it's the organism's natural defense
against the fear of its extinction
animals don't sleep when they're afraid
and neither should we
still a defense of anxiety may be mounted
on the grounds that you can convert it
to adrenaline as actors do on opening night
or parachutists who know fear is the greatest high

# JULY 19

∞

My idea of a critic
is the disgruntled
shoeshine man
in Albany who
slashed a bunch
of paintings (but
only the best ones)
in the government
mall, Governor
Rockefeller's "last
erection," so the
paintings had to be
restored, which cost
the taxpayers a lot
of money, and now
they are hung in
remote places where
they can't be seen

# JULY 24

∞

"If I had to go to military school
because one of you died
and the other was declared insane,
not that that would ever happen,
I know how I would deal with
the sadistic characters
who shave your head
and take away your individuality
When they challenge me
I'm going to say
I answer to the Lord only
and I might recite Psalm 13
or the song of praise in Exodus
and I'd keep on praying
It's no wonder God no
longer speaks to us
we aren't listening all we do is fight
still I feel in military school
you should have the right
to be a human being"

If your sestina about Sarajevo equals
mine about the cab ride in *The Big Sleep*
we have more things in common
than are dreamed of in your philosophy
as Hamlet didn't say to Horatio
your reticence being the flip side
of my apparent close-to-the-vestness
I know you hold the Ace of Spades
with a flush in hearts showing
and if I don't raise an eyebrow
when you add a blue chip to the ante
it's because there are more things
in your philosophy than are dreamed of
in heaven and earth and I should know
since I slept somewhere between the two
last night in a cloud that looked like
a melting iceberg but was warm
and firm as a trampoline

# JULY 31

Today I took a personality test
the guy told me to write down the date
and meditate
so I did it's the last day of July
and I wish it were thirty-one days ago
because I love July and want a year of them
aha, said Doctor Kampf,
why don't you look ahead
to thirty-one days of August pleasure?
because, I said, of Caesars I prefer Julius
that vaguely comical figure in Shakespeare
who gets off one really good line
"the valiant never taste of death but once"
to which Hemingway's life work is a footnote
ah well, our time for today is up
said Doctor Kampf and
what an entertaining pedant you are

# AUGUST 5

❧

*for Larry Kelts*

Smoke tumbled into the intersection
of Broadway and 23rd St., site of the insurrection
that failed for want of a human connection.
Who'd have thought the laws of reproduction
could have stirred up protests across the nation?
Where there's smoke, there's action,
and when the band plays "Tuxedo Junction"
we will dance like our parents in anticipation
of spring and the scent of lilacs at railway stations
across the great American depression. Our function
is to sing and dance and not worry about the coming election
of souls aspiring to salvation,
including some who were delivered by C-section
while the leader of the Calvinist faction
asked his wife to admire his morning erection.

# AUGUST 6

❈

On Charlie Simic's tape
of great girl singers from the 1920s
I love the song with the lines
you're wonderful
but I could be wrong
I think I'll write a poem
in which every second line admits
that I could be wrong I'll call it
"Poem of the Twentieth Century"
every line will begin with a year
1905: Einstein said light consists
of quanta & behaves like both
waves and particles
but I could be wrong
1964: Surgeon General declares
smoking hazardous to your health
but I could be wrong
Some say the century began
when you could measure either
the position or the velocity
of a moving object, not both,
I say it began in June 1948
but I could be wrong

Did you know
that today in 1982
the great American bull
market began and today
in 1997 it didn't end?
I wonder what else happened
fifteen years ago it was
the day Henry Fonda died
where was I
in New York probably, looking
for work a publisher asked
me to write *The Sinus Handbook*
"if you don't think you're too
literary for that"
and no one that day had ever
heard of St.-John's-wort or
feng shui or carpal tunnel syn-
drome what a long way we've come
the Dow closed that day under 800
and today it's under 8,000
and the Dodgers are a game
and a half out of first
it's hot and I'm eating a bowl
of gazpacho to quicken my thirst

The books on my night table
have titles on their spines
but the pages are blank
and I get to fill them in
today's title is *The Criminal Mind*
a thriller in which the Super Bowl
is fixed Buffalo wins and
the Dow Jones average goes down
as part of the scam
another book that waits to be
written is *The Riot Act* about
Montgomery Clift and Lee Remick
who fall in love while organizing
students in Michigan in 1961
and then there is *The Guest of Horror*
for the young adult market
which proves that wrath is the deadliest
of the seven sins so much to do
so many minutes to do it before
the saxophone seizes the melody
which becomes a dirge and the body
still on New York time adjusts
to the absence of traffic and noise
the steady drizzle in the garden

⬡

The romantic view of marriage
prevails in America with
the result (Bertrand Russell
wrote) of "an extreme prevalence
of divorce and extreme rarity
of happy marriages" that
was in 1929 and today it's truer
than ever I thought as I
drove down 17 and stopped
at the Roscoe Diner which
I called the Rothko Diner
by mistake with the result
that the walls were filled
with stacked rectangles
of saturated color S. calls
up and says he smashed the modern
icon in Illinois boy did I give it
to Rothko I said his pictures were
like postcards and on the back of each
is written "having a peaceful time
wish I were all here"

# AUGUST 18

If we knew then what I know now
I'd have written you love songs
with rhymes like "ex-mates
instead of sex mates"
we'd go to speakeasies in the 20s
skip the 30s
and take the subway from Brooklyn in the 40s
across the great divide
with the bridge behind us
we'd take a walk on Liberty Street
where I'd have an office and a secretary
and we'd get drunk every Friday night
and never get out of bed in the morning
we'd drink coffee and read the paper
for maybe thirty minutes and then go back
to where we came from and wake up
in a different decade
and it's still Saturday morning and the air
smells like August

# AUGUST 26

Ten brandy snifters are missing
and there's an air conditioner in my bedroom window
with a video recorder concealed inside
a power surge protector is missing
as is my favorite Sinatra CD with George Siravo
that's what I like about subletting my place
you never know what will be there and what not
when you get back from four weeks in Alligator Alley
two in the green hills of Africa and eight in Carthage
but (you ask) what was I doing in Carthage
like Marius among the ruins wearing sexy sunglasses
well, I was trying to sell them on our new line
of "Pardon Our Appearance" posters
and what do I need with ten brandy snifters
oh, reason not the need, I say
Lear being my anagram of the day
(for real) whoever you are reading this
you exist as do I in your magnificent ear

∞

Like coming to the end
of a very long novel
and finding out what
memory the hero has
suppressed, an ordinary
one, like the kid who
caused his parents'
divorce or something
awful he saw that
convicted the butler
of murdering his wife,
the boy can't find
his childhood it seems
he has misplaced it
with his father's bowling
trophy and his own
bottle cap collection
each tantrum ends
in the quietness of
a bride who is terrified
but loves him nonetheless

The anxiety was overpowering.
It didn't mean anything but
he knew he'd miss it if it were gone.
The first movement was like
a dance of horses at the Battle
of Borodino, where, on September
7, 1812, Napoleon defeated Kutuzov,
and Prince Andre, knocked unconscious,
woke up and wondered whether
he was dead. Music saved him.
He felt lighthearted listening to the
Academic Festival Overture but leaped
to his feet with the rest of the dons
when Brahms ended the frivolity
with *Gaudeamus igitur*. Then came
Schubert's Trout Quintet, then
Mahler's *pièce de résistance,*
"Frère Jacques" in a minor key.
Was this how he kept his sanity?
No, it was how he kept his vanity.

The word I object to in this poem is *sky.*
Every time she runs out of inspiration she falls back on *sky.*
I didn't like the title, "Sky Terrier." What the hell does that mean?
I liked the title but not the first line.
I was totally into it until then.
If you took out all the adjectives, you'd have a better poem.
I think she should substitute *Ohio* for every noun in the poem.
I love yellow there, the many words for yellow.
The loneliness of that color really got to me.
But why are the canvases huge?
I like the parentheses but I don't like what's in them,
especially *flame.*
Language aside, I like it from an emotional standpoint.
But you can't leave language aside.
Who says? It's my poem and I can do anything I want to it.
I just wish there were less *sky.*
It's become such a cliché in poems.

We have too much exhibitionism
and not enough voyeurism
in poetry we have plenty of bass
and not enough treble, more amber
beer than the frat boys can drink but
less red wine than meets the lip
in this beaker of the best Bordeaux,
too much thesis, too little antithesis
and way too much *New York Times*
in poetry we've had too much isolationism
and too few foreign entanglements
we need more Baudelaire on the quai
d'Anjou more olive trees and umbrella pines
fewer leafless branches on the rue Auguste Comte
too much sociology not enough García Lorca
more colons and dashes fewer commas
less love based on narrow self-interest
more lust based on a feast of kisses
too many novels too few poems
too many poets not enough poetry

# SEPTEMBER 12

The year I wrote obituaries
for a living I lived in
a small studio in the Village
listened to Coleman Hawkins and
walked fast I solved murders
in my spare time thanks to my
buddy Phil, a cop on the
homicide squad I had beers
with at the Cookery, women
were a mystery to me for
example there was the night
when Barbara (not her real name)
said she'd received a death
threat during a tarot reading
it was smokey when I got there
a candle shone in an empty jug
the Queen of Swords was curled
up on the couch, throat slit, and
when I went home with the no
sleep blues I had to write
eight hundred words on Robert
Lowell who died that day in a cab

Remember the '70s
when every poetry book
had to have a participle
for a title, i.e., *Running on Empty*
or *Fucking My Girlfriend's Roommate?*
I do. I also remember when
New York's tap water was the envy
of cities from Detroit to Los Angeles
and the best bagels could be made
only in New York as a result.
No longer. Now I sit around
and no one ever explains what
El Niño is. I mean, I know it's a storm
system all our weather is blamed on
but I bet as few people really
know what it is as know what
http stands for on the Internet
or the difference between the Internet
and the Web. Not that I care.
But I still want to know.

Thomas Hobbes, I thought of you
today on the FDR Drive if you
want a picture of man
or woman in the state of nature
watch the drivers shift lanes
without signaling and flip you the bird
and shake clenched fists and swear
and scream and honk it's every car
for itself and everyone's in a rush
to go home to nagging spouse
or empty nest or unmade bed
or stiff drink there are days when
nothing less than a dry martini will do

No bed so
I had to
sleep in the
synagogue it was
the end of
the last century
and our grandparents
rejecting the faith
of their fathers
had two choices
they could be
capitalists or radicals
in Russia on
Rosh Ha'Shanah what
would the right
choice have been

SEPTEMBER 22

∞

It's the day of the ram
and the head of the year
Rosh Ha'Shanah at
services I sat next to
Mel Tormé who outshone
all comers with his bar
mitzvah heroics while on
my left is Barnett Newman
big talker whose favorite
subjects include the horses
and the stock market he
knows the odds the women
are seated upstairs this is
an orthodox congregation
very serious I make
eye contact with the wife
of Menelaus who runs off
with Paris confident I'm Paris

## SEPTEMBER 30

I entered the elevator without ceremony
The guy in the gangster suit with the violin case
said "I have something to give you," toothily grinning
It turned out to be an orange pharmaceutical vial
but it contained ashes instead of pills
"These might have been yours," he said
It was day one of my hunger strike
and I don't expect you to admire me
O sleeping man, because of whom the sea is in an uproar,
it is your story I want to read aloud this afternoon
how you shipped out on the next freighter,
running away like a child determined to be caught
Where is your violin? Will your God save you now?
And they tossed him overboard, thinking he would die
It was a challenge he welcomed, for he did believe in God
though he did not believe in atonement and forgiveness
bread and wine for some, bread and water for the masses
expelled from the cathedral or kept in a cage like a sideshow freak
and the elevator doors snap shut behind me

Reading the paper
was a luxury
I couldn't afford
today, not that I
lack the sixty cents
but the time divisible
into units of sixty
I can't leave the
office until 49 E-mails
and 13 phone calls
test the merits of
each medium I missed
the whole Yankee
game (1–1 entering
the 10th) as I walk past
Gray's Papaya on the
way to today's version
of my American
Dream, a pair of
brown shoes in
a shopfront window

# OCTOBER 11

Of cities I know New York
wins the paranoia award
the place you'd least like
to be stuck between floors
on a temperamental elevator
on 14th Street or ride on
the N train when the
conductor's face is missing
that must be why we like it
we who like to think we
thrive on risk on the other
hand the discrepancy
between the cold air
outside and the overheated
flat is without parallel and
completely without justification

∞

My bag was missing at the airport
"Just one bag?" "Yes, but it meant a lot to me"
I had seen the bartender before, but where?
"You didn't tell me you had been to Oxford"
"Yes, I was at Magdalen College for two years"
"What did you do there?" "Drugs"
"Did you know that in Hindi the same word
(*kal,* pronounced 'kull') means both
yesterday and tomorrow?" "You don't say.
What'll you have?" "Bombay martini straight up,
with olives, very dry and very cold." "I like
a man who knows what he wants." "Well, I'll
tell you. She was a handsome, self-assured woman,
a practicing physician, 48, bright, in great shape,
played tennis every Friday night,
didn't drink, smoke, or take drugs,
and was looking for a Romeo with brains.
So naturally I didn't phone her"

Before I read your
poem, dear Charles,
I'd have planned on
Keats at second base
Shelley at short
Wordsworth in center
Coleridge in left
Byron at first base
John Clare in right
Leigh Hunt at third
Blake catching and
Whitman a surprise
starter on the mound
with Poe available
for short relief
in Yankee Stadium
where the October shadows
lengthen in left field
as Yogi Berra once put it
it gets late early there

I asked Nixon why
he hadn't demanded a recount
in 1960 when dead
voters in Illinois and Texas
put Kennedy over the top
"I figured we got cheated
fair and square," Nixon said
I asked him about Kennedy's
assassination he didn't want
to talk about that but nodded
when I said "Cuba—he was
killed because of Cuba, right?"
Nixon wanted to talk about
his most humiliating public
moment I was surprised "it's
not what you think," he said
it happened in 1960 when he
stammered "America can't stand pat"
and now he wondered whether
his wife will ever forgive him

# OCTOBER 23

Nikki phones and asks
me the difference
between a synecdoche
and a metonymy and I say
"he's a prick" is an example
of a synecdoche, the part
standing for the whole
oh Nikki you bring out
the beast in me also the
beats in me but now I must
erect an edifice complex
in the capital of my mind
and dedicate it to you
dear Nikki who must write
a poem every line of which
ends with wow

∞

My watch is beating
but my heart is fast
this morning I'm like
a kid on the way to
Ebbets Field to watch
my heroes lose to
the Yankees with my
father to console me
afterwards I need
Horace Silver to play
a song for my father
that he can hear and
delight in his son
on the tenor sax
pouring out the night
wherever you are, Dad,
I hope you're listening

# OCTOBER 25

∞

It's the opening movement
of Mendelssohn's Italian Symphony
so this must be New York City
in 1972 I am walking up Amsterdam Avenue
to hear my favorite medievalist lecture
on Chrétien de Troyes my favorite
was Yvain the moment when the hero
after bedding his beloved must
negotiate a transition back to
his commitments as a knight a familiar
problem in my own experience
which also explained John Donne's idea
that love makes one little room
an everywhere the world suspended
within a benign parenthesis from
the moment of turning out the lights
to the moment when that busy old fool
unruly sun makes a racket outside
and the day wakes up and the lovers
go their separate ways everyone says
graduate school sucks but I'm reading
Auden, Freud, and Lionel Trilling
and I have my date with the Italian
Symphony to look forward to

Today I decided
Bill Clinton is
the Tina Brown
of politics
the magazine is
in the red but
it's the talk of
the town the biggest
collage of celebrities
and meritocrats this
side of the Inferno
(trans. Robert Pinsky)
I remember when Jack Jones
sang the commercial for
the Chrysler New Yorker
in 1975 when Carlton Fisk
hit the homer it's the
beautiful New Yorker (he
sang) it's the talk of the town

Remember when Khrushchev said
"We will bury you!"
on the cover
of *Time*
I thought he was
employing a metaphor
as in "Braves Scalp Giants!"
on the back page
of the *Daily News*
I pictured the Russians
burying us under a mound
of all the rubble
that roubles could buy
when what he meant was
he came not to praise Caesar
but to bury him

Since you asked, dear Larry,
this is how I met Arthur Miller on
a late September evening
two months after taking Joe,
then ten, to see *A View
from the Bridge,* not knowing
how much it would upset him
Barbara phoned and invited me
to have dinner with her and Larry Rivers
and if I had known Arthur Miller
was going to be there I wouldn't have been
the last to arrive we had coq au vin
he was tall and talked about Clifford Odets
Brooklyn and Michigan
Larry called him Artie
Marilyn Monroe's name never came up
and I got to tell him
my favorite line in *Death
of a Salesman,* "it's not enough
to be liked, you've got to be well liked"

The bridges that make Manhattan an island
and Brooklyn part of another island
I sing
as Joe and I cross the Williamsburg Bridge
on the way back from our tour of the Brooklyn Brewery
where Joe asks whether it's true that atoms must be split
to make beer no not atoms but molecules do
and hops are added in the last five minutes for their aroma
and to counteract with bitterness the excess sugar
we sample the brews Joe favors the wheat beer I the Belgian ale
and afterwards we are walking down Seventh Avenue
and Joe says he loves the city because
he has to walk fast to keep up with his old man,
and the funny thing is the same is true for me

Not just vanity, a symptom of disorder
and self-deception, but the cool predicament
of the actor conscious of his role in the drama
who dies before the final curtain drops
the vice president of sales so orderly in his days
so punctilious in his duties yet how ridiculous
in his three-piece suit and watch fob
drunk with lust for a woman half his age
he, too, has his dignity though filled
with self-disgust as he clambers down
the crisscrossing ladders of the fire escape
leading to an alley littered with half-eaten refuse
and leaves the scene of the crime undetected

# NOVEMBER 13

∞

*for Mark Stevens*

I want your opinion
of my manuscript
my friend because
you know Art
and I know Art Linkletter
but you have a deadline
to meet while I have a date
with a certain great novelist
in my apartment
whose idea of heaven is the men's room
of Grand Central Station
and hell a prison in a posh suburb
with a swimming pool where
you can feel like a fly in a highball
you read one sentence and you know
the number of martinis
that went through that
system is not to be
counted on an ordinary abacus

∞

Taxicab yellow
the red of a burst blood vessel in the eye
a pint of carrot juice with ginger
this is what I have to work with today
and "the power to die," a phrase
in both Tennyson's "Tithonus"
and Emily Dickinson's
"My Life had stood—a loaded Gun"
the door opens but no one walks in
something brushes lightly against his skin
the professor is still talking
but the text has changed
the background music has become unstable
and anxious, as if it could avert
a catastrophe by announcing it,
and I will never know the name
of that symphony I heard
once and once only

Who wants a mass-market audience
I just want a mass-market bankbook
with a little privacy and enough energy
for all the days of the year
as they come, stay awhile, and leave
with Bartók's *Pieces for Orchestra*
on the radio as the windows darken
just before evening arrives
I want this moment, no other will do,
to conceive of great debates between
the self and the soul
battling it out in verse
the self fluent as a sestina
the soul reduced to seventeen syllables
the self a cosmos or a public frog
the soul a self-described nobody
the self getting in the last word
the soul content with a laugh

∞

In  Ezra Pound's novel *1984*
England's  prime minister
is Weinstein Kirschberg
and the American president
is a Jew named Rosenfeld.
Mussolini is strung up
by a mob. Hitler plays Risk
in his bunker. Stalin
makes threatening phone calls
to citizens chosen at random.
The novel's hero has just enough
time to woo the haughty heroine
and steal the celebrated bust
of Homer from the Nazi official
who filched it in Italy. But
there is no escaping the secret
police. They are everywhere.
They tap his phone. If they capture him
they will put him away for life. They're
hot on his trail. They're almost there.

# NOVEMBER 19

∞

*for Beth Ann Fennelly*

Do I still like to think
of myself in the third
person? I do, I mean,
he does. He liked, too,
to read the paper on
the couch with a cup
of coffee in his robe
daydreaming of a girl
he hadn't met who
liked doing a pirouette
in an ankle-length
silvery gray skirt
that flares in a full
circle when she does so.
Not that she planned
to do so onstage, but
it was nice to know
she could. She thought
of herself as a fair warrior
on the strand hearing
the warring voices
of the sea, and he was
her demon lover, who
liked sitting around
dreaming of the things
he liked, like the girl
who shoplifted lipstick
because she liked
the sound of its name.

Went to "The Waste Land" last night
Fiona Shaw's one-woman show
in a derelict theater
on West 42nd Street it was
the first poem of the 20th century
in which bad sex is a metaphor
for the failure of civilization
which is searching for a place
by a placid lake where it can have
a nervous breakdown in peace and quiet
the first poem of the 20th century
to resemble a crossword puzzle
the clues in the form of fragments
phantom quotations and the image
of Eliot in a bedroom with a monastic bed
and a single unadorned lightbulb
in the ceiling he was the straightest-
looking poet of the 20th century
with a superb cover, a banker's
three-piece suit, but he was as crazy
as the rest of us, with rats and bones
and dry rocks rattling around his brain
and a drowned sailor's swollen eyeballs

∞

I used to think other people's
lives were more real than mine.
Journalists covering a war could
talk about truth and commitment
in an open-air jeep, smoking.
Movie stars could run for Congress
on a rock and roll platform
and I could make fun of them but
secretly I envied the woman next door
who went to her office every day
where she "pushed papers and crunched
numbers," she told me, without
explaining what that meant. But
she felt part of the great extravaganza,
Thanksgiving, Christmas, the works—
in love on New Year's Eve,
by Valentine's Day brokenhearted—
while I stayed in my apartment
searching for words to describe
feelings that had already departed.

# NOVEMBER 28

∞

*with Stacey Harwood*

Mia and Mark I want to welcome you to
the association of alcoholic aphorists
the brotherhood of bards
the congress of charismatic correspondents
the diaspora of diarists
the *école* of ecstatic essayists
the fraternity of flaming fabricators
the guild of guilty timewasters
the hordes of horny haiku-slinging whores
the institute of ink-stained inditers
the jury of jaded journalists
the kangaroo court of critical opinion
the league of literature's loopy lovers
the *maison* of masturbating memoirists (e.g., Joyce Maynard)
the nation of nervous narrators
the organization of obfuscation
the prisonhouse of impenitent plagiarists
the Quonset hut of quotable queers
the republic of wry raconteurs
the society of scribes
the tea party of the literati
the union of the underrated
the vault of the vilified versifiers
the wretched ranks of real writers
the Xanadu of eccentric experts
the Yugoslavia of yesterday's youthful Yaddo-goers
and the zero-sum game of Zeus and zeugmas

Is it time for the woman to turn
to the man and say, "It wasn't
supposed to be like this?" No,
because this isn't a spy movie,
it's just me in my new fedora and
double-breasted navy trench coat
with high winds of up to forty miles
per hour pushing me forward to
East Fourth and Second Avenue,
the KGB Bar with its red walls
and framed posters of Revolutionary
Russians, for poetry reading number nine
of the season. Last year anyone got
a free drink who could answer why
the hottest New York nightspots
(e.g., Pravda) were named after defunct
Soviet institutions but no one got
it right and now it's time for the man
to turn to the woman and tell her
that she's the olive in his martini

# DECEMBER 2

∞

*for ARA*

The last man in America
without a telephone answering machine
lives in a haiku in Sonoma
or a house on Cayuga Heights Drive
where his poems take daily walks
observing the morals and manners of
natural beings cruel in their kind
and kinship to us while the mind
of man, superior to all he surveys,
is in repose, subdued by medication,
a fit subject for a painter of the day
this day when something unusual
happened, like Auden marking
the death of Yeats on his calendar
and ours, if poetry makes anything
happen it's in your head the mind
in motion on the page in verse
that should not be interrupted
so I'll let my machine take that call

# DECEMBER 4

∞

I'm not in love but I'm higher than
Freddie Hubbard at the Blue Note
espresso spiked with brandy
light cream and brown sugar
and you (who are not who
you think you are) start
philosophizing about sex
between grown-ups which
you liken to a conversation
I can hear it now
the man says I'm looking
for a one-bedroom
in the West Village
the woman says
there's one on Cornelia Street
for $145,000 and
low maintenance
that's what it's like in New York
and three apartments later
they're ready
for a cigarette in the dark

DECEMBER 7

∞

Rhyme *wave* with *leave*.
Postpone diet.
Do not do today what you can
as easily not do tomorrow.
Do not lend your car to a friend
of a friend. When you get it back,
you will need a new solenoid switch.
Mourn quietly. Drink lots of liquids.
Watch parts five and six of Dennis Potter's
*Lipstick on Your Collar.*
Read up on the Suez Crisis of 1956
and what it meant for "Little England."
Was the invasion really known
as "Operation Musketeer"?
Do not answer the phone.
Do not comply with alternate
side of the street parking regulations.
Do not remember Pearl Harbor.
Whatever you were going to do,
don't do it. No need for a handshake.
Just wave and leave.

# DECEMBER 9

It was when I was waiting for you
to turn up as I knew you would
as you always do
that I felt like the spy at the end of the novel
who dies with his German girlfriend
at the British Museum
or with his English girlfriend
at the Berlin Wall
then the music changes
it's Art Tatum and "You Took Advantage of Me"
they didn't die after all they're still alive
in a café on a beach in Venezuela
on a special deal, four days for $995
though their luggage got lost, arousing their suspicions
and meaning they had to do without their clothes
for the first twenty-four hours
which wasn't so bad
as they had some catching up to do in bed

∞

There's an old French saying,
"the whole of a man's mystery
rests in his hat," and if you
translate it into American
you get Sinatra smoking
and singing "Memories of
You," "I Thought About You,"
"You Make Me Feel So Young,"
and "You Brought a New
Kind of Love to Me," all
from the same 1956 session,
I love that voice and have since
the summer I was eight and
my friend Ann and I sang "Love
and Marriage" on Talent Night
at the bungalow colony when I'm
down there's nothing like you,
birthday boy, singing "All of Me"
to lift me up and when I'm in love
I jump out of bed in the morning
singing "It All Depends on You" and
your voice comes out of my mouth

## DECEMBER 14

This bed thy center is, these walls, thy sphere,
The tarnished, gaudy, wonderful old work
Of hand, of foot, of lip, of eye, of brow,
That never touch with inarticulate pang
Those dying generations—at their song.
The One remains, the many change and pass
The expiring swan, and as he sings he dies.
The earth, the stars, the light, the day, the skies,
A white-haired shadow roaming like a dream
Limitless out of the dusk, out of the cedars and pines,
Think not of them, thou hast thy music too—
Sin and her shadow Death, and Misery,
If but some vengeful god would call to me,
Because I could not stop for Death,
Not to return. Earth's the right place for love.
My playmate, when we both were clothed alike,
Should I, after tea and cakes and ices,
Suffer my genial spirits to decay
Upon the bridal day, which is not long?
I thought that love would last forever; I was wrong.

DECEMBER 16

Writers write books because
they're unsatisfied with the ones
they can buy, so I, liking the idea
of a big city daily that people may read
as they sip their coffee and chew on
their donuts, must create it for them,
granting them the pleasure of jumping
from the sight of an olive-backed kingbird
to the building of a domed stadium in Flatbush
in my paper one article reports a guilty verdict
an adjacent article declares the opposite
there are no op-ed columns or editorials
the comics are in French the crosswords in Spanish
the opera reviews in German the sports in Esperanto
and the date on the front page changes daily
today is December 16, 1997 yesterday was
December 7, 1941 and tomorrow the treaty
will be signed in a railway car in Versailles

In the great fox versus hedgehog debate
that Isaiah Berlin sponsored—
the hedgehog who does one
thing versus the fox who does many—
I come down firmly on the side of the fox,
and today's manuscripts, letters, faxes,
E-mails, and succession of phone calls
overlapping each other like a version
of serial monogamy proves it: any day
beginning with a phone call from John
Ashbery is a good one and then there was
lunch with Glen at Bruxelles, chapters
of my book to photocopy, a new title
for these poems (*The Daily Mirror*—
like it?), and why am I so exhilarated?
as if the blood in my veins ran as fast
and recklessly as the traffic down Fifth
and the lights in the top story windows
shine in rooms where I am writing

∞

I haven't published my first issue yet
and already the letters to the editor
are coming in: outrageous that Burger King
is quadrupling the amount of sodium in their fries,
kudos to the guy who stole an NYPD tow truck,
and why is it that they can land a man on the moon
but when a train is stuck the whole subway system
is frozen? Also, now that winter is around
the corner, let's remember our little friends,
the squirrels: bring a bag of yesterday's bread
with you, and some nuts, when you go to the park.
I am a Vietnam vet and wondering whether there is
any decency left. Who does this guy Farrakhan
think he's speaking for? Good riddance
to Judge Murphy, since who else should be held
accountable for their decisions if not judges? All
the bleeding hearts on the Upper West Side will
not bring one victim back to life. I say,
bring back the electric chair, the sooner the better.

To return home
after a long journey
and read the mail
and know you were
thought of on days
you didn't think
you knew anyone
in European cities
where spies exchange
briefcases in cafés—
seeing you is like that
after six months of not
seeing you on a Sunday
afternoon in an under-
heated, overpriced
Manhattan flat with
Betty Carter, "I'm yours,
you're mine," on the
radio at two-fifteen

Christmas defeated Chanukah
once again last night
by a margin of three billion dollars
or so, but every time I hear
a Yiddish word like *bubkes*
in a movie (*L.A. Confidential*)
or when Oleg Cassini in that new play *Jackie*
calls a garment a *shmatte,* it's "good
for the Jews," as our parents used to say.
Meanwhile some things have
stayed the same; the drunken lout
in the street is still somebody's father.
Hey, kid, how does it feel to have a pop
that's a flop? And we had such good ideas
for changing the mental universe, if only
as a project in philosophy class, the one
I still dream about failing when I have
that dream everybody has, of being back
in college and needing this one course
to graduate, which I forgot to attend

I spent a month writing love poems
to women I didn't know (see May 7),
women I had met for a whole half
hour (August 18), fictional characters,
composite dream-drenched figures,
and all for the pleasure of being
a French poet in prewar Paris, having
a Gauloise and an espresso on the run,
I had vast metaphors to make,
no sooner did I have an idea than
I would witness its fulfillment,
a tower or a bridge, and head on
to the next project and of course you
were there with me the whole time
though unnamed in the rain as if
nothing could be more romantic
than a shared umbrella

# DECEMBER 31

It's the year's midnight and almost the day's
and I'm in a good mood because
I was having drinks with the vice president
of Brooklyn Brewery, makers of Brooklyn Brown Ale,
importers of terrific raspberry-flavored Belgian beer,
and sponsors of this poem
also present were Nora, a classicist on her way to Bulgaria,
Renee, a nonclassicist on her way to Ithaca,
and Barbara, a costume designer heading for Martha's Vineyard
and guess which one likened the boom in poetry
to the boom in microbreweries
we'll drink to that
in an apartment belonging to Ruth, a retiree in Delray Beach
the weather was like April on Sullivan Street
and the voice on the radio said
"everyone wants to go to heaven
but no one wants to die"

# ACKNOWLEDGMENTS

Grateful acknowledgment is made of the publications, print or electronic, in which some of these poems first appeared, in several cases with titles instead of dates: *Boston Book Review, Boston Review, Boulevard, Brilliant Corners, The Cortland Review, Jacket, Lincoln Center Theater Review, Lingo, Lit, Michigan Quarterly Review, Nerve, New American Writing, The New Republic, Pharos, Ploughshares, Poetry Daily, Shenandoah, Slate, Sonora Review,* and *Verse.* Of the thirty poems that *Poetry Daily* posted on its Web site in April 1998, nineteen are included here. A few dates had to be changed in cases where more than one poem worth saving was written on the same month and day.

Mary Jo Bang, Mark Bibbins, Amy Gerstler, Stacey Harwood, and Robert Polito read different versions of this manuscript and made me improve it. I am grateful to them, to Glen Hartley and Lynn Chu of Writers Representatives, and to John Fontana, Joy Jacobs, Giulia Melucci, Erich Hobbing, and Jay Schweitzer of Scribner. To my editor, Gillian Blake, I owe a special debt, and perhaps the largest one, for her encouragement and astute advice.

Made in the USA
San Bernardino, CA
21 October 2013